Faith B...

MOM

Is there a mom in existence who couldn't use a little extra advice when it comes to living out her faith in front of her kids? Maria Holmen, with a little help from her husband, Mark, has written a concise, practical guide on this subject that every busy mom will appreciate.

Yvette Maher
Senior Vice President-Family Ministries, Focus on the Family

As a senior pastor, Mark Holmen demonstrated how a local church can inspire and equip families to instill strong faith in the next generation. As a partner in the Strong Families Innovation Alliance, he has also been a mentor to other leaders trying to turn the tide of declining generational faith transference.

Kurt Bruner
Executive Director, Strong Families Innovation Alliance

Mark Holmen is energizing families to grow their faith in the home. Mark and his message is one of the freshest and most practical voices among Christian leaders. This resource is helping us follow the mandate of God to pass on our faith from generation to generation.

Jim Burns, Ph.D.
President, HomeWord
Senior Director of the Center for Youth and Family at Azusa Pacific University

Mark Holmen clearly knows what spiritual development in the family should look like, and he knows how to communicate that message in a warm, transparent and engaging way. Parents who digest the four Faith Begins @ Home booklets will have their vision lifted, their hearts warmed, and their minds focused on the practical things they can do to see their children embrace Christ for a lifetime. I recommend these resources to every believing family.

Richard Ross, Ph.D.

Professor of Student Ministry at Southwestern Seminary
Fort Worth, Texas

Mark Holmen is providing much-needed leadership in the Faith@Home movement that is sweeping our nation. These resources are excellent tools in that they both challenge and equip parents as they seek to disciple their own children.

Steve Stroope

Lead Pastor, Lake Pointe Church
Rockwall, Texas

Maria & Mark Holmen

Author, *Faith Begins at Home* and Founder of Faith @ Home Ministries

Faith Begins @Home MOM

Regal

From Gospel Light
Ventura, California, U.S.A.

Published by Regal
From Gospel Light
Ventura, California, U.S.A.
www.regalbooks.com
Printed in the U.S.A.

Library of Congress Cataloging-in-Publication Data
Holmen, Maria.
Faith begins @ home mom / Maria and Mark Holmen.
p. cm.
ISBN 978-0-8307-5231-7 (trade paper)
1. Mothers—Religious life. I. Holmen, Mark. II. Title. III. Title:
Faith at home mom.
BV4529.18.H65 2010
248.8'431—dc22
2009046388

1 2 3 4 5 6 7 8 9 10 / 15 14 13 12 11 10

Rights for publishing this book outside the U.S.A. or in
non-English languages are administered by Gospel Light Worldwide, an international not-for-profit ministry.
For additional information, please visit www.glww.org,
email info@glww.org, or write to Gospel Light Worldwide,
1957 Eastman Avenue, Ventura, CA 93003, U.S.A.

I dedicate this resource to my mom, the source of hope I draw upon to do right by my child. The example she has set will be handed down for generations to come. What a great way to say "I love you" to your child. You're my rock, Mom. Way to go!

Contents

Introduction

I looked in the mirror with the pregnancy test in hand, and an overwhelming thought rushed over me: "I will never be the same again." Then I cried. I cried tears of happiness for what was to come, and tears of sadness for what had been. Mostly I cried tears of fear. What were we thinking! We didn't know how to parent. What if God didn't bless us with the ability to do this? What if He had other gifts in store for us, but not this one? What if no one helped us? What if we failed?

My husband, Mark, had never changed a diaper, baby-sat, or even longed to hold someone else's baby. As a pastor, Mark looked with terror at the congregation each time he dedicated a baby. There would be a hush across the sanctuary as he would gingerly and clumsily hold the baby up for presentation. Would this be the time he would drop the baby? Of course he never did.

I was just as clueless about babies. I had worked all my life in office jobs, and even in high school when most girls my age were baby-sitting, you never heard me say, "Oh, what a cute baby. I wish I had one."

Malyn Mae Holmen entered the world like many other children. She was put on my stomach, and Mark instantly started to touch her and talk to her. He was completely caught up in the moment. I could see and hear him doing the things I should be doing, but I knew that as soon as I touched her, she would have me, heart and soul. She would consume me. She would become the gift God had given to me, and I would never be the same again. I was right.

About two years later, I was on the phone with my mom when Malyn came waddling by. She was in her yellow pajamas with the feet. She was chewing on her toothbrush. She went over to the dog, sat down and leaned back on the dog as if the dog were a pillow, kicked her legs out and crossed them and smiled at me. I suddenly said, "I would die for this child!" My mom answered with a tone that I will never forget. "I know how you feel. I've always told you that you are the best thing I have ever done, and now you know what I mean."

A mom moment. A little glimpse of heaven right here on earth. It was a moment that Mom had been waiting for since the first time she said, "I can't wait until you have your own child. Then you'll understand." Now I understood.

You don't really know what God is up to when He gives you a baby, but if you grasp the wonderment and become engaged in the ride you have begun, this journey will be the best you have ever taken. This booklet is part of that journey through God's Word as you discover what He has in store for you and your children. You are not alone on this parenthood journey. Moms everywhere can have God's Word to guide and direct them. Throughout these pages you will come across "Mom Moments for You." Take time to reflect honestly about your experiences and allow God to shape you into a faith-at-home focused mom.

Mom Moments for You

- What went through your mind when you first discovered you would be a mom?
- How prepared did you feel to be a mom at that point? How do you feel now?
- How has becoming a mom changed you or your perspective on life?
- What is one piece of advice you would give to a mom-to-be?

1

Enjoying a Long Life

These are the commands, decrees and laws the LORD your God directed me to teach you to observe in the land that you are crossing the Jordan to possess, so that you, your children and their children after them may fear the LORD your God as long as you live by keeping all his decrees and commands that I give you, and so that you may enjoy long life.

DEUTERONOMY 6:1-2

"Prepare today so you are ready for tomorrow" was the motto at our house when I was growing up. There was never a time when we weren't looking to the future for finances, school and work. Mom and Dad dedicated themselves to making sure my brother and I were equipped, to the best of our ability, to live productive, law-abiding lives. They passed on the "good stuff" and always had their eyes and ears open to "new stuff" that would help us. They essentially handed us the commands, decrees and laws, teaching us so we could pass them down to our children and our children's children.

Did my parents actually think about what they were doing? Did they ponder for long periods of time about this? Make major lists of things to cross off? Wonder about each situation that would come up? Wrestle with the end goal? No!

My parents were what the Bible calls equally yoked. They had the same priorities. They knew what they wanted for us with very little discussion, consultation or research. They knew because of what had been passed down to them. It was what they wanted us to have or not have because of things they had been through. It was the breaking of some cycles of life that should not be passed down and the forming of others that should. It was natural yet intentional.

Mom Moments for You

- What are some things from your childhood you would like to pass on to your children?
- What are some things you do not want to pass along?

Faith from the Heart

I want to speak mom-to-mom right now, urging one thing of you: Get to a place where the faith your children develop flows from your heart to theirs. It is the foundation they will need to build the rest of their life. The best way to do this is to pass along the "commands, decrees and laws the LORD your God directed me to teach you" (Deuteronomy 6:1).

Equip your children for living a long life. God has clearly given you the things you need to be a good mom. God has told you the things you need to pass on, and it is your job to make sure you pass the right things on to your children. If you don't take the time, effort and love it takes to teach your kids from birth forward, how can you expect them to handle the future and all its wonders and complexities? That would be like handing them the world in their tiny hands and saying, "Here you go. Good luck with it, and by the way, I love you so much." It's easy to focus on teaching your children what they need to succeed here on earth and neglect teaching them God's ways, commands and decrees. Yet God has a much greater purpose in mind for you and your children. They are precious to Him. He has chosen you to train them for Him. He will prepare you to do it.

"I know the plans I have for you," declares the LORD, "plans to prosper you and not to harm you, plans to give you hope and a future" (Jeremiah 29:11).

Be careful to do what the LORD your God has commanded you; do not turn aside to the right or to the left. Walk in all the way that the LORD your God has commanded you, so that you may live and prosper and prolong your days in the land that you will possess (Deuteronomy 5:32-33).

Even the very hairs of your head are all numbered (Matthew 10:30).

Mom Moments for You

- What is your greatest hope for your children?
- What is your greatest fear?

Intentional Sharing

God made your children, and He wants what is best for them. He wants to spend eternity with them and with you. Think about that. Is your purpose to do your best so your kids will enjoy life on earth only? Or is your purpose to do your best so you can enjoy a long eternal life in heaven together?

If you haven't caught this by now, this is not a casual conversation or feel-good mommy moment. This is a huge deal and a huge responsibility. Setting your child on the right path is the best thing you will ever do, remember? The outcome is calculated. It is direct. It is precise. It is intentional. It is bottom-lined. Now your life is about intentionally and diligently following God's ways and teaching your children the ways of God so that they (your children and your children's children) may enjoy long life.

What does intentionally showing your child how to live God's way look like? It looks like tiny steps taken every single day. It requires joyfully showing and telling them some of the same things over and over. It is being transparent with them from day one so they not only understand what the goal is, but they will also desire it themselves. It starts with the faith in your own heart. It starts today, whether your children are tiny or taller than you are.

- Let your children see you read God's Word and pray.
- Tell your children how you are growing and learning new things.
- Enjoy getting together with other believers.
- Pray with your children every day. Begin today.

I gave a gift to Malyn from God when she was around two years old. Over the years Mark and I have also benefited greatly from it. It started when we went to a class for parents at church. There we heard a story of how a man and his wife had blessed their child almost every night from childhood through college. It was a moving story of connection, hope, love and commitment. It was a practice we vowed to incorporate at our house. As soon as I got home, I wrapped up my sleeping little bundle in her favorite blanket and rocked her in a rocking chair that had been handed down to me from generations before. I have often wondered how many times my mother rocked me in this same fashion in this chair. I brought my child's little face up to mine and, cheek-to-cheek, I gently breathed, "May God bless you and keep you. May He make His face shine upon you and be gracious unto you. May He give you peace. In the name of the Father, Son and Holy Spirit. Amen. I love you so much."

I didn't know then what complete joy it would give me each night I blessed her or how this simple thing would transform our family. I just wanted her to be connected with God; and in turn, I got to be connected with her. Every night, even as a 13-year-old now, Malyn announces, "I'm ready for bed now." Like little soldiers called out to duty, Mark and I stop whatever we are doing and march into her room. She is snuggled down with the dogs on either side of her, waiting for the end of her day's routine. I give her the blessing that God has given me to share. Mark prays with her. She never worries about how her day will end. Even when our time together during the day has been less than stellar, we always come together as a family and end it well. It rinses the day away and sets us up for a new tomorrow. Even when we are apart from each other, one last phone call includes the prayer and blessing.

This is a nonnegotiable at our house, although it sometimes requires a little bit of creativity. Once Malyn traveled by herself to attend Bible camp with some of her friends in another state. One of the camp rules was no phone calls to or from home. What about our nightly blessing? I bought a card for each of the 14 nights she would be gone and wrote her blessing for each night. Mark did the same with his cards for the prayer side of things and we put them in her suitcase to open each night. Even though we couldn't hear her sweet voice every night, our connection was not broken. She knew that even though we could not physically touch her, we could still touch her life.

Today, Malyn regularly blesses us out of the blue. She sends her father off on speaking trips with a blessing. She texts us blessings for no specific reason. Do you know what it is like to be blessed by your child? Your heart wants to leap out of your body and scream, "Yes! Thank You, God!" And what brings me even greater joy is knowing that if she does this with us, she will do it with her kids when she becomes a mom. One day she will sit in that same rocking chair and say to our grandchild, "May God bless you and keep you. May He make His face shine upon you and be gracious unto you. May He give you peace. In the name of the Father, Son and Holy Spirit. Amen. I love you so much." That's enjoying long life here and making preparations for eternity.

Mom Moments for You

- What is the most important thing you could teach your children?
- How do you plan to teach your children the ways of God?
- What is one thing you can start doing today that will lead to you, your children and your grandchildren enjoying eternal life together?

2

Listen and Practice

Hear, O Israel, and be careful to obey so that it may go well with you and that you may increase greatly in a land flowing with milk and honey, just as the LORD, the God of your fathers, promised you. Hear, O Israel: The LORD our God, the LORD is one. Love the LORD your God with all your heart and with all your soul and with all your strength. These commandments that I give you today are to be upon your hearts.

DEUTERONOMY 6:3-6

The word "hear" is used several times in this passage. It means more than to hear the words being spoken. It means to really listen, to absorb what is going on, to read between the lines, to think and ponder how to incorporate into your life what you have just heard.

I spend a lot of time hearing what God has to say in the quiet times when I am in my car, at my desk or in the few minutes I have to myself in the bathroom as I get ready in the mornings. Through my walk with God, my time hearing Him seems to come at unscheduled times, in moments that steal into my mind. I try to trap these thoughts for further consideration and application. For me to hear, I need silence or involvement in mundane tasks so that my mind is freed up. Maybe you're like that. Maybe you're like my husband, Mark.

Mark likes noise. He functions well with noise. If Mark is along there will be noise that goes with us too. The first time I saw him study in college, the books were spread out, the radio was on and the television had a ballgame on with the sound off. Three things were going on at the same time he studied, and he still received great grades and top religion student honors when he graduated. Not me. It was silence and solitude when I studied. Sometimes I would study in the bathtub in the dorm restroom because everyone took showers instead of baths, and so no one could find me to disturb me.

Whatever your noise preference is, have ears ready to hear God's message to you and for your family. When God says "hear" in this Scripture passage in Deuteronomy, He does not want to be background "noise" that fills our lives. God wants you to hear what He has to say to the point that it forms action in your life and your children's lives. When Moses twice says, "Hear, O Israel," he is making it stand out so that His people will pay attention to the particular things he is saying next and put them into practice.

Mom Moments for You

- How do you best "hear" from God? What are some things that help you get closer to Him?
- Has God ever had to get your attention? If so, how did He do it?
- When you hear the word "obedient," what thoughts come to mind?

Obeying God's Ways

One of my favorite parts of this Scripture passage is "Hear, O Israel, and be careful to obey so that it may go well with you" (Deuteronomy 6:3). Obeying is big for me. I am an all or nothing kind of person. I am either doing it all the way or not at all. Unfortunately, this set me up to be a person that was either very regimented or not at all involved. I was either obeying or I wasn't. It was black or white. Yet, in the last five years, I have evolved from a strictly black-or-white type of gal to more of a gray. Can you still obey and live in the gray? As long as it is rooted in the foundation of the truth, you can. Let me try to explain with a practical example.

Have you ever struggled with your weight? I am not talking about having 5 to 10 pounds to lose. I am talking about a battle with your weight, being in the trenches, wanting to strangle this enemy and end the misery once and for all. I am one of those warriors. The extreme of my emotions can be seen around my middle and thighs. When I go through something that stirs up my emotions, I put on weight. When I have a settled time in life, my weight is under control.

When Mark became a senior pastor for the first time, it was an emotional time. We left family and friends to start a life that God had truly called us to. That alone didn't stop my many trips to the fridge. One year later and carrying 60 additional glorious pounds, I was a form of myself I did not know and did not like. It was at that point that I simply looked in the mirror and said I don't want to do this anymore. I was finished with being a yo-yo, with my up-and-down weight reflecting my emotions.

This year will be my fifth year as a thin person. I have taken off and kept off 50 of the 60 pounds and manage each year to get the last 10 off just in time to get on the boat in the summer. Those 10 pounds are my gray area. Am I still "obeying" my health goals? Yes, to the best of my ability. On a daily basis, for most of the year, I am not going to forget what it takes to keep off 50 pounds. But a regimented life that includes keeping off those last 10 pounds all the time is not worth it.

Do I obey my plan? You bet! Do I drive myself crazy with the rules? I'd rather enjoy the foundation and freedom God has given me and see His wonders rather than getting caught up in always focusing on the boundaries.

So what does this have to do with being a faith-at-home focused mom? When it comes to teaching your kids to "be careful to obey," you need to live it out. But be alert or you will lose the forest because you focus only on the trees. You are human and so are your children. No one is perfect. Don't require perfection from your kids. Create a home environment where you are continually learning how to be more careful and more obedient. It is a continual process. When you mess up, admit it. When your kids mess up, teach them to go to God for forgiveness and to move on. Here are some ways to create a home environment that encourages faith and obedience.

1. Young Children
- Every day, tell your kids "I love you," and pray for them.

- Tell your kids that God wants to hear lots of thank-yous (see 1 Thessalonians 5:18). Throughout your day, say, "Thank You, God, for . . ." Encourage your children to repeat what you say until they are saying it on their own.

2. Older Children
- Write notes of encouragement and put them where your kids will see them.

- Talk with your kids about what you can do as a family to learn more about God and how to live for Him. Write these ideas down and pick one or two to do together.

3. Teenagers

- When your kids struggle with following Christ, remind them to forget what is behind, strain toward what is ahead, and "press on toward the goal to win the prize" for which God has called them (Philippians 3:14).

- Require all family members to be kind to one another. God is kind to us. In fact, it is His kindness that has brought us to Him (see Romans 2:4), and He wants us to be kind to others (see Ephesians 4:2; Colossians 3:12). What your teens learn at home, they will take with them as they share their faith with others.

I love Poet Maya Angelou's famous words: "When we know better, we do better." Doing better requires knowing better first. If you want your kids to live a more obedient and godly life, you need to help them know a more obedient and godly life.

One of the things that Mark points out when he speaks at conferences is that many parents today want to be good, God-honoring, obedient parents. Unfortunately, many are not able to do so simply because they do not know how. That is due to the fact that most parents today did not grow up in a home where godly living was modeled through prayer, Bible reading, devotions or worship in the home. That was the case for me. My parents loved God, but we didn't talk much about our faith in the home. Now I have a home of my own, and just because the best was not modeled for me does not mean all is lost. My parents did their best with what they were given. Faith at home was not something that was emphasized when they were raising my brother and me. But we know better, so now we can do better.

So, "Hear, [insert your name], and be careful to obey so that it may go well with you." You have an opportunity to know and be better, no matter what type of environment you were raised in; but you need to listen up and you will need to obey. This decision will not only impact you but it will also affect your children your children's children. It is a requirement from God that has a benefit: "Be careful to obey so that it may go well with you." Choosing to obey and teaching your children to obey is worth it.

Mom Moments for You

- How would you rate your level of obedience at this point? In what areas do you want to improve?
- What is a spiritual area you are stronger in than you were 10 years ago? What is one area you hope to grow in over the next 10 years?
- What are you doing so that you can know God better 1, 5, 10 years from now?

Pass It Along

Some of the first memories I have of my dad are of him praying by the side of the bed every night. He would get down on his knees, clasp his hands together, put his forehead on them and simply pray—just a time between him and his God every night. No matter what had gone on during the day or what time he was finally going to bed, he always took time to kneel and pray. At a very young age, I learned my first prayers with my father kneeling beside me at my bed. To this day, I know that he still gets down on one knee, even with physical limitations, and prays. I know that he is not only praying the standard prayers that God gave us, like the Lord's Prayer, but his own prayer for me and mine, for my brother and his, for my mom and for anyone else who needs it. While we didn't pray a lot together as a family, Dad's example to obey and teach his children the Lord's Prayer connected me to God.

So now what am I going to do? Have I passed the importance of prayer and the Lord's Prayer on in exactly the same way? No. I don't get down on my knees at night. But there is rarely a silent moment in my life when I am not praying, and my daughter knows it. In the car, before I go to sleep, in the morning, on the boat, before meals, it doesn't matter. If we travel past an accident on the road, we instantly pray for the people in the car.

We just pray all the time. There are many times we pray the Lord's Prayer together. We have grown in our obedience to prayer by increasing the number of ways and times we pray together. Malyn now knows how to pray at mealtime, bedtime and anytime. She will take it with her as she grows and has kids of her own. I can't wait to see the creative ways she will pray with our grandkids. It is only going to get better. When we know better, we do better!

Mom Moments for You

- What example and teaching for prayer and spiritual living was given to you as a child?
- What spiritual examples and teaching are you passing along? What would you like to do more of?

Choosing God's Ways

The final part of the Scripture passage reads "Hear O Israel; The LORD our God, the LORD is one. Love the LORD your God with all your heart and with all your soul and with all your strength" (Deuteronomy 6:4-5). These two verses make two very important points.

Your children have many mind-boggling options. They get hit from every side with solutions, gimmicks, lies and truths. As a mom, my radar is super keen to the best way to maneuver through all of these options with my child, especially in spiritual matters. Believe me, I have gone into stealth mode with this since Malyn is 13 and seems to be bringing more information to me than I am to her lately. Yet one constant in our house never changes: We believe in only one true God—Father, Son, and Holy Spirit—and we love Him with all of our hearts. We never pull parts of things from different religions or beliefs or manmade truths together to make up our foundation. And while I'm sure this isn't the politically correct thing to say, when it comes to my daughter's eternity, being politically correct is not the issue. There has to be a time when you draw a line, and when it comes to there being one true God, it is one of those times.

In Matthew 5:37, Jesus says, "Simply let your 'Yes' be 'Yes,' and your 'No,' 'No,'" meaning there will be times as a mom when you will need to say yes and no. And while this may sound strange at first, I have found that as children grow, equipping them to say no is a great thing because it gives them a sense of being, and helps them live out their convictions with confidence. Training your child to be firm takes time and requires open discussion about what is and isn't acceptable. It involves taking the time to listen to your children when they bring information and questions to you, and having open discussions. It is also means taking time to bring issues up with them.

I am finding that parenting an older child is different from parenting an infant. When Malyn was young she needed me for nurturing and general hands-on care. Those needs have diminished and instead I'm spending far more time with her and her friends. We have become a "hub house," where Malyn and her friends hang out. I often find myself in the middle of their conversations and activities. A lot of times I wonder why they would invite me into their conversations. The primary role I usually play is to be a steadying force in their unsteady world. Many times I am simply a sounding board or reminder to help keep them focused on doing life God's way. In a world of so many options, they need a place to turn to and find what is truly right and wrong.

That's a role you get to play as a faith-at-home focused mom. You get to be a steady and reliable source of information that will help your kids say yes and no to the things of this world. Yet, if you keep changing what you think is right and wrong or what is acceptable and not acceptable it becomes increasingly difficult for your children to choose. At an age when my daughter and her friends could be pulling away, we are instead reinforcing our commitment to the Lord and His ways here at the Holmen home.

Begin teaching your children to choose God's ways no matter what age they are now. Teach young children that just like they do what you tell them to, you do what God tells you to do. As your children grow older, read the Bible with them and write out in a notebook verses you come across that tell you how to live God's ways. Look for ways your teenagers are following God's ways, and let them know you notice it.

Mom Moments for You

- Do you believe there is only one true God? How do you keep other beliefs from infiltrating your faith?
- Do you love this one true God with all of your heart, soul and strength? How do you express that?
- Are you living in a consistent way that shows you are consistently following and obeying God no matter what?

In Love with God

When you understand there is one true God, who loves you, who has a plan and purpose for your life, who gave His life so that you, your children and grandchildren may enjoy long life, loving Him with all your heart and with all your soul and with all your strength almost becomes second nature. Reflect for a moment.

Beating someone over the head with a stick doesn't make him or her love you. The same is true about the way you are going to impress your kids to be in love with God. Letting someone see what your life is like with God as the center will win way more battles with your kids then force-feeding it to them. Loving our one true God is something that is caught rather than taught.

Never did I doubt who was the one true love of my Grandma Dorothy. Oh, she loved her family and friends, and we all knew it, from the special ice cream bars in the freezer to the time spent visiting neighbors. But her first love was God. She served the Lord, and we all knew it. She lived her life devoted to him. How did we know? By her actions. She didn't talk about it as much as show us, from the Bible verse plaques in her house, to the Jesus statues in her garden, to the number of times she went to church services and served there, to the way she talked.

My sweetest memory of her was staying on the farm with her and Grandpa while my folks had a date. I was probably eight years old, and I could not fall asleep. I finally got up enough courage to cross the hall and stand at the side of Grandma's bed. I just stared at her until she awoke with a start. She was so kind as she took me back to bed and asked if I wanted her to lie down beside me. She prayed out loud until I fell asleep. It is a memory I will always remember because she showed me how much she loved her God. To this day, when I have a hard time falling asleep, I still say the Lord's Prayer over and over and over and think of Grandma Dorothy.

Mom Moments for You

- Are you living "in love" with God?
- Does your lifestyle reflect that you are "in love" with God?
- Would your kids say that you are "in love" with God?

3

Impress Them

Impress [God's ways] on your children. Talk about them when you sit at home and when you walk along the road, when you lie down and when you get up. Tie them as symbols on your hands and bind them on your foreheads. Write them on the doorframes of your houses and on your gates.

DEUTERONOMY 6:7-9

Words! What would you do without them? Think of how much time you spend using words in one form or another. You read them, communicate with them, manipulate them, rejoice with them, cry with them, annoy others with them, create with them, impress with them, sing with them and love with them. Even when no one is around you can have a meaningful conversation with yourself using words.

We have a dog that joined our household about 4 years ago; he "speaks words" to us. His name is Sota (named after our love for Minnesota), and he is a character. When he comes inside or wakes up in the morning, he has to find something to carry around in his mouth—a sock, pillow, bone or leash. He prances up to each one of us and "speaks" to us with this thing in his mouth. It is a happy little muffled, whiny bark. He is proud of himself and expresses, "Look at me!"

And what do we do? We talk back to him. "Oh, big boy, such a big boy, what you got? Tell us your story!" You can hear the same phrases come from each room he enters until he has seen each of us. These words somehow reinforce Sota to keep strutting his stuff around the house. Eventually we stop speaking and he stops prancing. He is finished and happy. He has been recognized and talked to in words he has no idea the meaning of, and he has told us a story we don't know the meaning of, but we still all communicated. He has been impressed with this routine in all its craziness.

The Routine of Words

This passage in Deuteronomy is about the routines of communicating with your children. "*Impress* them on your children. *Talk* about them when you sit at home and when you walk along the road, when you lie down and when you get up" (Deuteronomy 6:7, emphasis added). What you say is being impressed upon your kids. The meaning of this part of the verse is that there is no time when we should not be incorporating communication about God with our kids. A little daunting? Tempted to set this book aside and forget the whole thing?

You can be overwhelmed to the point of not doing anything, or you can just get started somewhere doing something. It is God's commandment to you as a mom. To be honest, getting overwhelmed is not an option. Getting overwhelmed is like saying to your child, "Since I think I might fail at this, or I don't want to look foolish in front of you, or I don't have time to add one more thing to my plate, I am not going to try at all." Sorry, not acceptable.

Start small. It doesn't matter if the only thing you start with is saying a prayer before a meal *every* time you eat, or asking your child when he or she jumps in the car *every* day, "Hey, any blessings God showed you today?" Or waking her up *every* morning with a small prayer of thanks for the day that is to come. Did you catch the key word, "every," in each situation? Develop routines.

When the journey begins between you and your kids, it has to be intentional and regular. Without the intent, the nonnegotiable behavior, the "stick to it" determination, any plan will fall away like all great things that start on a Monday with gusto and end on Saturday with a fizzle. You don't need to rely on your own resources, though. Jesus says, "Remain in me, and I will remain in you. No branch can bear fruit by itself; it must remain in the vine. Neither can you bear fruit unless you remain in me" (John 15:4).

You may be just beginning parenting with your newborn. It's not too early to start impressing. Your kids might already be teens. It is never too late to start—ever! It may not be easy. You may get the rolling of the eyes from them. They may think you have lost your mind. They may even tell their friends that you are "going through some midlife thing, because guess what we are doing at home!" So what! The foundation has to start sometime, and the longer you wait, the harder they will fight. In the end, they will need to make their own decisions about their faith. You have a job as a mom: raising them to see and hear God's ways through you. Start building faith-talk into your everyday conversations with your kids.

- Begin your days saying a simple prayer out loud in the presence of your children: "Thank You, God, for another day to serve You on earth." "I love You, Jesus, and all You created." "Direct my steps through to-day, Lord."

- Notice the homeless man begging at the corner and say, "Let's pray for him because we don't know what his story is." And then pray for him.

- Walk into your cleaned children's rooms and tell them how much it honors you and God when they respect the things that have been provided for them.

- Comment about the healthy choice your child made to have an apple for a snack, and how proud you are and God must be for taking care of the body He gave them.

Live out your faith in front of your children. Once the faith language has been well established, start to add new ways to encourage spiritual growth in your children. With young children, it is easier to live your faith in front of them. They are sponges taking in all you are sharing. It will simply become a part of their lives. It will become their "normal." With older children, you will have to stay the course. You will have to fight for these kids! Eventually, they will come to know that this is how you are going to talk at your house from now on, and after a long period it will become normal for them. Will there be trials and tests to see if this is going to stick? Yep. Will the devil be pushing you from every angle to give this up? You bet. Don't quit! In the end you, with the help of God, share the gift God is trying to give them. Wouldn't it be too bad if the gift was never given because you thought handing it over was too hard?

Encouragement Through Words

I'm not much of a reader, never wrote much. I'm an introvert, so I'm not big into conversations with lots of people. Speaking in public has never been a great desire of mine. I don't like to talk on the phone, don't do any "social networking" on the computer, barely do emails. But I like words. I like encouraging words. I like small sayings that make me want to shout "Woo-hoo!" or give me the strength I need to get through something. I have developed a habit over the years. I rip encouraging statements out of magazines or write them out and tape them to the mirror in our bathroom. When I brush my teeth in the morning and again at night, I read these words. I impress the positive statements in my head so I can remember that all this stuff I am doing (mostly mom, wife, exercise stuff) is worth it. Each summer, when we get back from vacation, I tear the sayings off the mirror and start all over again. Here's a sample of the current sayings on my mirror.

- We're living up to our name.
- The only thing harder than a morning run is a day without one.
- Celebrate the simple.
- Unbeatable.
- Want to fit into your skinny jeans?
- The hardest part is to decide.
- And my favorite right now: It's time we girls cooled off more and freaked out less! Enough said.

At the beginning and ending of *every* day I can choose to get bogged down in all I have to do or I can rejoice in all I have been given to do. I get to do it for God and for the people I love. Words of encouragement can impress you to choose the right way even if it is hard. Encourage your children with your words and teach them to commit God's Word to memory. Here are some words you might want to impress on your children on a regular basis until their message becomes a natural way of thinking.

1. Young Children
   · God is right here with us. You are never alone.

   · God hears you every time you talk to Him.

2. Older Children
   · You have gifts and abilities that God wants you to develop as you grow up.

   · You really touched my heart when you said or did that.

3. Teens
   · You are becoming such a responsible young adult. I like how you carefully consider your choices and then make wise decisions that please God.

   · Love God with all your heart and soul and mind and strength. Fall in love with Him before you fall in love with another person. He will make all the difference in your relationship.

Search Institute conducted a nationwide survey of more than 11,000 participants from 561 congregations across 6 different denominations. The results were revealing:

- Only 12 percent of teenagers have a regular dialogue with their mother on faith/life issues.

- Only 9 percent of teenagers have experienced regular reading of the Bible and devotions in the home.[1]

As a faith-at-home focused mom, you have to make faith-talk a part of your everyday conversation. You can't take your kids to church and expect the church to do it for you. You have to talk to your kids about God and faith and what that means in the way you live. You don't have to say a lot and you don't have to be an expert on the Bible. If you run into a question or situation that you don't have a biblical answer for, simply say three very powerful words, "I don't know." Then over the next couple of days go search out the answer from a pastor or Christian friend or study Bible. Your kids will learn that you are a lifelong learner too.

Mom Moments for You

- Did you have faith-talk in your home as you were growing up?
- When and where did you engage in faith-talk growing up?
- What are some times and places you can have faith-talk with your children?

Beyond Words—Faith in Action

The second part of the Deuteronomy passage, "Tie them as symbols on your hands and bind them to your foreheads. Write them on the doorframes of your houses and on your gates" (6:8-9), gets specific about how to live your faith. It is not saying you need to rush out to the Christian bookstore and buy up all the latest and greatest paraphernalia to display so your kids know you mean business. It does not mean you show up at school to pick up your kids with shirts that read, "Jesus rocks and my kids do too!" Not every word from your lips needs to be surrounded by quotes from the Bible or covered in syrupy sweetness.

Rather, let your actions speak volumes. Don't just rely on words. Show me a family that enjoys each other's company and praises God before stepping out the door to go to school each morning, and I will show you Deuteronomy parents who have writing on their doorframes and gates. Present to me a child who goes down to the local food pantry or mission and hands out food to the homeless, and I will show you parents who have tied symbols to their hands. Bring to me a family that has banded together with other families to paint an elderly person's house as a service project to serve the Lord; show me a parent who shows up *every* Sunday to serve as an usher or greeter at church with a genuine smile; let me see a parent who makes a big pot of soup *every* Friday for the nearest shelter to hand out to the homeless. Those are the homes that are passing on their faith through their actions to their children. What you do to "impress" the decrees and laws God has given us can take on many forms.

Over the past 16 years of serving churches, we have come to know many families. Each family is different, but all have had common goals. I have never met parents that didn't want the best for their children. I have learned that being a Christian does not mean being a perfect person living a perfect life where everything turns out perfectly. While I already knew that Christians make mistakes and have imperfections, I soon realized that serving God does not prevent us from experiencing sorrow and heartache in life . . . and sometimes from decisions our children make.

My husband and I have watched many imperfect families, just like us, passing their faith to their kids in all sorts of intentional and creative ways. We have dealt with families as they experienced depression, alcoholism, divorce, abuse, physical and mental illness, deaths, destruction, teen pregnancy and suicide. And yet these families have kept living obedient, faithful lives.

Time has passed, and we are now receiving invitations to graduations, weddings and adult baptisms of some of those young people we knew as little children. We know about the struggles their parents went through over the years of raising them, but we also know that in most cases they were doing the best they could to pass on God's truths to the people they loved.

The bottom line is that incorporating God into your life will help some things but it doesn't always fix everything, at least not right now. But your staying strong through adversity makes a huge statement to your child. While loving God does not mean life is always going to be rosy, maintaining your faith through adversity leaves a lasting impression.

Mom Moments for You

- What "actions" impressed you to become a Christian?
- What "actions" can you engage in weekly or monthly to impress your children to live as Christians?
- Has there ever been a time when you began to lose faith? What strengthened your faith again?

Shaping Faith

What does a life of impressing others through word and deed as expressed in Deuteronomy 6:7-9 look like? My father-in-law, Arlen, devoted his life to sharing God's Word, especially with young people. He served the church and was a camp director at a Bible camp for over 20 years. Even though he served God faithfully, his family went through many trials. Even so, the message God had put him on earth to give was never weakened.

Here's how Mark puts it in his book *Faith Begins at Home*: "On the surface we were a strong Christian family of five that included my parents and two older sisters. My dad was a camp director and my mom was an incredible person whom many called a living angel. A lot of people thought we were the perfect family. Yet little did they know that behind the scenes, my dad was a closet alcoholic."[2]

Arlen was able to battle his demons and was sober for the last 18 years of his life. I only knew him in the final years of sobriety. The first time I met him was in an interview for a position as Waterfront Director at Riverside Bible Camp. I thought it would be fairly simple. What questions could be so hard about running the pool and the staff that went with it? I already had my Senior Lifeguard certificate and had passed all the tests for the State of Iowa to be qualified for the job. Arlen didn't care much about that. He wanted to know about my walk with Jesus. What was my faith was based on? What would I be passing on to the campers that summer? It was an eye-opening experience. The camp experience that followed changed my life. My faith was well-grounded, traditional, stable and had taken root. It was a good start, but I had yet to really take it out for a walk. There was a lot of that summer that was uncomfortable for me as I tried out my new "faith-walking shoes." I learned that my faith and walk needed to be visible both in word and deed. But there would have never been that experience without Arlen's guidance.

Arlen took ill around the first of 2004, and after a time, Mark was called back to Minnesota to be with his Dad. I received a phone call from Mark as he thought they were in the final stages of saying good-bye. He asked if Malyn and I would like us to relay anything to his dad. I sat our 7-year-old, Malyn, on my lap in front of the computer. She dictated what she wanted to say and I typed for her. Mark read it to his dad before he passed away.

October 23, 2004

Dear Papa,
I hope you are feeling better. I miss you a lot. Take care of Daddy. Say hi to Jesus for me. Hopefully the water is wet in heaven. Eat some extra bezet and licorice for me.
   I love you!
   Love Malyn

We cried together remembering her Papa the way she saw it. They had always teased each other about how water isn't really wet. "Bezet" is a word she made up with Papa that meant dessert, mainly because Papa loved anything sweet. She had had talks with Papa about Jesus and she felt comfortable wishing him well in his new life. My letter reflected the way Arlen had helped shape my faith walk as well. Here are some excerpts from what Mark shared with him from my heart.

Dear Arlen,

I have had the privilege of knowing you for almost 15 years now, and I wanted you to know that my life is richer for the experience.

You were the first person to show me Christian unconditional love. . . . I believe it was the beginning of my walk with the Lord. . . . God blessed you with the ability, drive and desire to be that "somebody" for people. I can't think of a higher calling, or a greater gift to be given. . . .

Your willingness to accept me as part of your family (to the fullest) has always amazed me. There are always times when we are unlovable by our actions, our words or our circumstances, but it is nice to know that there is a circle of people that love and accept you no matter what. . . .

Back on March 30, 1967, you and Myrne added a son to your family. Four months later, I was born to my loving family. I love how God weaves lives together and makes them become one. I praise God for every day I get to spend with YOUR son here on earth. I have never loved anyone more . . . until YOUR grandchild was born. Without a doubt I treasure these gifts. Family ties weave such a deep bond and the bonds that you have woven through your children WILL be passed on to your grandchild. She will hear all the camp stories. She will hear all the family stories. . . .

I am SO glad that you passed on the dream of heaven, the roads of forgiveness and the unconditional love of God to so many while you were here. . . .

Your one and only daughter-in-law (and Riverside Waterfront Director),
Maria Karolena Holmen

Arlen is the one I think of when I reflect on the Deuteronomy 6:7-9 passage. Arlen passed away in November 2004, and the following June, Malyn and I spent a week with my folks in Iowa. Malyn and my dad were sitting on the front porch when a truck drove by that transported ice creams and desserts. My dad said to Malyn, "Hey, didn't Up North Papa love ice cream?" Malyn said "Yeah, the truck stopped all the time." My Dad looked at her and said, "Let's go then!" and they ran down the street to catch the truck, purchased a box of ice cream bars, sat on the front porch and toasted

Papa as they ate ice cream and talked about him. What a sweet celebration of a life lived for God!

In the end, we can get so wrapped up in life that we miss the opportunity to "impress" our children. We choose to not invest in one of the most important things we can pass down for generations to come. It doesn't have to be overwhelming, but it does have to be intentional. Eventually, intentional leads to natural. A natural faith walk with your children is what I will be praying for you!

Mom Moments for You
- Who are the people that God has used to shape your faith?
- What are some life experiences that God has used to shape your faith?

Notes
1. Reprinted with permission from *Effective Christian Education: A National Study of Protestant Congregations.* Copyright © 1990 by Search Institute SM. No other use is permitted without prior permission from Search Institute 615 First Avenue NE, Minneapolis, MN 55413; www.search-institute.org.
2. Mark Holmen, *Faith Begins at Home* (Ventura, CA: Regal Books, 2006), p. 10.

4

Be Careful

When the LORD your God brings you into the land he swore to your fathers, to Abraham, Isaac and Jacob, to give you—a land with large, flourishing cities you did not build, houses filled with all kinds of good things you did not provide, wells you did not dig, and vineyards and olive groves you did not plant—then when you eat and are satisfied, be careful that you do not forget the LORD, who brought you out of Egypt, out of the land of slavery. Fear the LORD your God, serve him only and take your oaths in his name. Do not follow other gods, the gods of the peoples around you.

DEUTERONOMY 6:10-14

The Legacy of a Mom

My mom spent all of her life making sure that my brother and I succeeded one step further than she was able to. She desired to make the most of life and to be thankful for what she had been given. My brother, Wade, and I both had great high school experiences and graduated from college. Our lives are now surrounded and supported by family and friends. If you ask Mom what she is most proud of, it would be the legacy she is leaving as a mom. Mom

broke down all kinds of walls and barriers to raise
Wade and me in a house filled with love.

She did it with two underlying factors: (1) We
could always come home, and (2) we could always
ask for and receive the truth. These are two genuine
heart gifts from a mom. Now, could we always come
home to stay forever? To hide out? No. Why? Our
place was never to stay with our parents forever. But
the safety and comfort of "going home" is like a
warm, cozy blanket you look forward to wrapping
yourself up in when you get home from a long, hard
day at work. It is much the same as when I look forward to spending time in Iowa with my folks. Time
almost stands still when I sit out in the shop with
my dad or fix supper with my mom. We all assume
the same roles as we did when I was a teenager living on the farm. We always ate at a long bar with
four stools in the kitchen. We each always sat at the
same place.

The first meal that Mark ate with us at the
farm, he did not know about our assigned places,
and when he got his plate, he sat down on a stool. I
told him that was where Mom sits, and he couldn't
sit there. Of course, Mom didn't care where she sat,
but I did. Even as a grownup who had moved away
to college, coming home meant things never
changed much, and I didn't want them to. This passage in Deuteronomy is a gentle nudge for you to be
careful and not forget where you came from and
who helped you get where you are.

In Deuteronomy 6:10-12, God spells out all the wondrous things you have to rejoice in. They are simple things, like land with cities, houses filled with good things, wells, vineyards and olive groves. What more could you want? They are not the complicated things we have made them to be today. What God originally provided was all the good things you need to live and eat. He wants you to remember where all this came from in its purest form. He provided it all. What is the big deal about remembering it anyway? When you forget to acknowledge who gives you your gifts and blessings, the magnitude of those gifts diminishes. They can fade to the point of feeling like you were owed these things, and then you forget what it took to make them. That is why I started out this chapter about my mom. One of the reasons I am a faith-at-home focused mom is because my mom chose to model that to me. She gave me the foundation of love and courage to tackle things I never thought I could, and she did it the old-fashioned, simple way.

Mom Moments for You

- What was the foundation in your home as you were growing up?
- What was modeled for you at home that you want to model for your children?

Simply Model

What is the simple way to share your faith? I don't hold the only key to this. All I can tell you is what was taught to me, because that is how I live today. Growing up, I was required to work hard and do my best. How did Mom get this across? With lists, of course. From as long as I can remember there was a list on the counter. Some lists were for her, some were for the farm, some were for Dad, and yes, some were for us kids. We had daily things to do that never made the list, like making the bed, helping wash dishes, weeding three rows of the garden each day and feeding the animals.

The lists guided us through our additional tasks and taught us responsibility. My brother and I always had "equal" lists, meaning we each had the same number of things on our list. It didn't always mean things were equal. Wade's list may have included mowing the lawn, which took four hours; mine might have been to hang out the laundry on the clothesline, which took 10 minutes. The key was that Mom would go off to work and we would have all day to get the lists done. We could choose when we wanted to accomplish our tasks.

Usually, I would do the items on my list right away so I could have the rest of the day to do what I wanted. Wade would wait until the last minute, barely getting the list done by the time Mom's wheels hit the driveway. There was one theme as we grew up: We were *all* in this together as a family and *all* the members contributed.

My mom was not there to serve us, not because she didn't want to, but because if she did everything, we would have never learned simple life skills we needed to live life in the future. Working hard and appreciating what you have is the gift my folks gave us. Here are a few creative ways that Mom encouraged responsibility.

- I wanted contacts at age 14, and my mom said I could "earn" them by jumping rope. I was a basketball player, and the coach had told me that if I wanted to get lighter on my feet, jumping rope was a good way to do that. So my mom took that information and turned it into an opportunity. For every 100 jumps, I earned 3 cents. My contacts cost $200, and so I had to jump 666,667 times in order to pay for them. It took me a long time, but I did it. Because I had earned the contacts with blood, sweat, and tears, I never lost my contacts—and I had really good basketball seasons.

- Sometimes Mom would ask for an hour of time from each member of our family, and we would attack the house to get it clean. The hour we donated equaled four total hours of time that it would have taken her to do the work alone.

• Sometimes when supper was done, Mom would guess how long it would take to clear and wash the dishes, and then I would guess. We would set the timer and race around like crazy people clearing, washing and drying dishes. She made work fun.

Am I doing the same with my child now? Here's what happens at our house: Every morning Malyn is required to take the dogs out, feed them, make her bed, shower, get her things ready for school and make her lunch and breakfast. She does all this before heading off to school, and I don't have to ask her to do any of it. These are the things she does to help out our team here at home. Does she have lists of additional tasks? You bet. Do we ask her to work hard? Yes. But we play just as much because we all pitch in to get our work done.

Children of any age can contribute to the household. Here are some ideas to teach kids of different ages to work hard and get the work done. Don't expect perfection, but do require them to do their best and to do the job right. Give lots of encouragement and thank them for their contributions.

1. Young Children
• Let young children follow you around and "help" with the household chores. Give them a duster and tell them what good helpers they are. Tell them God likes their hard work.

- Get young children into the habit early of putting things away before getting out something else.

2. Older Children

- When you give your children a task, write out the steps or draw pictures so they know exactly what is expected of them. Add boxes in front of each step so they can check each off as they complete it.

- Gradually increase responsibilities. Tell them you are so glad you can count on them to do more grownup tasks.

3. Teens

- Give your teens a list of tasks to be done and let them pick two or three.

- Sometimes offer to work together with them on the chores. These can be opportunities to listen and talk while you work.

Teaching your kids to work and do it joyfully reminds them of all that God has provided. These provisions are gifts that need to be taken care of. My mom got stopped on the street one day by a lawyer in our small town of Montezuma, Iowa. He was raising teenagers, and he commented to Mom how much he had enjoyed watching Wade and me in high school. He asked her quite earnestly, "How did you and Ed raise such good Christian citizens?" She replied without even thinking: "You look them in the eyes every day and tell them you love them. You make them work. And you turn off the television." That's my mom!

Mom Moments for You

- How are you similar to or different from your mom?
- What is something you find yourself doing and saying that reminds you of something your mom would say or do? How do you feel about that?
- What are some character traits you hope to instill in your children? How would you like your children to be like you?

Living in the Moment

Deuteronomy tells you to remember when things were simple but your basic needs were met. Remember when you struggled and God promised to deliver you out *and* give you blessings? Jesus promised this, too, when He said to seek first His kingdom, and He would provide all you need (see Matthew 6:33). Take one day, one moment, at a time. The big part of the passage in Deuteronomy is "don't forget."

At our house we are choosing to call it "moment living." It's something rather new for us because we found we weren't doing it very well. After years of being brought up to plan ahead (a gift) and years of striving to get ahead (determination), somewhere we forgot to breathe and soak in all we had been given. It is taking a lot of practice for Mark, Malyn and me to really notice and appreciate all our blessings. We make ourselves stop in our tracks and verbally give praise. We thank God for the closeness we feel to Him, the house we live in, the cars we drive, the sunsets, the dogs, our friends, our family and on and on.

We are doing it not just with our family, but with others as well. Do you know how your attitude changes when you take time to notice and also thank the Creator of it all? It is uplifting, and the little things in life melt away. Moment living is tough to make a habit, and it takes time, but the benefits we are seeing at our house are truly paying off.

Another thing that we are doing in our home is a teen Bible study. God put it on my heart to gather some of Malyn's friends and get together once a week to hang out and go through a teen Bible study. At this age, they are starting to acknowledge God for what He is doing in their lives; talking about it will set them up to be comfortable talking about their faith as they grow into adulthood. We pray, do the study and write down our SMADS in a notebook.

SMADS is our code name for "smiles" and "mads." These are the things we pray about. We write down smiles, blessings, the good things that happened or that we are looking forward to. We write down mads, prayer requests, the things we aren't particularly excited about or that are just a plain bummer. We have added a weird category for things that don't fit in either category. Each week we look at our notes from the last weeks to see if there is anything that happened with those SMADS, and then we pray for the new SMADS for the week. I have girls sitting on my counter with chips and sour strips talking about stuff I never would have at their age. But they are comfortable, and at the end of the day they give all these requests and praises to God. I have to say, even if I go into Bible study tired and worn out, it always ends up the best time I have given to my daughter all week and we all come out feeling refreshed.

One of the things we have talked about quite a bit in our teen Bible study group is following the one true God. "Fear the LORD your god, serve him only and take your oaths in his name. Do not follow other gods, the gods of the peoples around you" (Deuteronomy 6:13-14). The girls and I have talked about Scientology, yoga, horoscopes and other spiritually borderline stuff. We have talked about others they know who believe a little of everything to make up their belief system. We have wrestled with the whys and we have talked about what people make up to worship. We have explored where these "combo meals" of faith take people. The conclusion of these 13-year-old girls is that all of it misses the mark. The "be careful" part of the Deuteronomy passage is that you really have to watch what seeps into your belief system and you have to watch what you pass on to your kids. They are watching who (or what) you give all the glory to. Make the choice easy for them; pick only one . . . the only one true God.

Mom Moments for You

- What SMADS (smiles and mads) are a part of your life today?
- How well do you do at living in the moment?
- What is something, at this moment, you want to give God thanks and praise for?

5

In the Future

In the future, when your son asks you, "What is the meaning of the stipulations, decrees and laws the LORD our God has commanded you?" tell him: "We were slaves of Pharaoh in Egypt, but the LORD brought us out of Egypt with a mighty hand. Before our eyes the LORD sent miraculous signs and wonders—great and terrible—upon Egypt and Pharaoh and his whole household. But he brought us out from there to bring us in and give us the land that he promised on oath to our forefathers. The LORD commanded us to obey all these decrees and to fear the LORD our God, so that we might always prosper and kept alive, as is the case today. And if we are careful to obey all this law before the LORD our God, as he has commanded us, that will be our righteousness."

DEUTERONOMY 6:20-25

The promise of this passage is given with a reminder to review the past and look toward the future. It is refreshing to hear that once we were slaves, yet the Lord delivered us. It is heartwarming to be reminded that the Lord sent miraculous signs and wonders—great and terrible. It is encouraging that He kept His promises of deliverance because of obedience. The beginning of this verse is the question we have been answering throughout this book. "In the future, when your son *asks* you, 'What is the meaning of the stipulations, decrees and laws the Lord our God has commanded you,' *tell* him."

From an early age, children begin to ask why. They are sponges, curious about their world, receptive to your instruction. You are forming the foundation they will continue to build on. As children grow, they process the experiences of life—good and bad—and add new understanding to the framework. When they become teenagers, they move into a new phase as they develop their own faith separate from their parents and start making decisions based on their values and understanding of the world and their purpose in it. Here are some ways you can help your children develop faith through the various life stages.

1. Young Children

- Give your children an understanding of what God's relationship is with them.

- God created and formed you before you were even born (see Psalm 139:13).

- God is like a shepherd who takes care of his sheep. He makes sure you have everything you need (see Psalm 21:1).

- God wants you to talk to Him about things that worry you(see Psalm 55:22).

2. Older Children

- Make it clear to your children that they are God's special creation and He loves them more than His own life (see John 3:16). God has many riches, and He lavishes them on His children (see Ephesians 1:7).

- Teach your children to go to God, confess and receive forgiveness when they mess up (see 1 John 1:9). And teach them to forgive others as they were forgiven (see Colossians 3:13).

- Teach your children that no matter what bad things may happen, God is always good. He never changes. We can find protection with Him (see Psalm 34:8). When things seem unfair, remind them that God "is the Rock, his works are perfect, and all his ways are just. A faithful God who does no wrong, upright and just is he" (Deuteronomy 32:4).

3. Teens

- Remind your teens that God will guide them in their decisions as they trust in Him (see Proverbs 3:5-6).

- When your kids face troubling situations, encourage them to look to God (see Psalm 46:1-2). Remember with your teen other situations God has gotten them through.

- As your teens branch out in new ventures, remind them they are not alone (see Joshua 1:9). God will help them become all He created them to be.

- When your kids are wondering where God is in difficult situations, point them in God's direction and help them see God working in ways that may not be so obvious (see Deuteronomy 4:29).

Talking with your children about these things is a process that happens over the years. As you deal with situations in your life or watch what others are going through, you will have many chances to ask and answer questions that will help build faith in your children.

Mom Moments for You

- Review your past. What has God done for you in your life?
- What Bible verses have special meaning to you? Why are they significant?
- How can you share these verses with your children?

Keeping Communication Open

Isn't the end goal to have the kind of open communication where your children will ask and you will tell? These key decrees and laws are what your children are going to need for the rest of their lives. They will need them to rejoice in the good stuff and get through the rough stuff, because life is going to have both. As this Deuteronomy passage suggests, getting through the rough stuff is sometimes the only way to see the really good stuff.

My adventure as a mom has astounded me. If anyone had told me I would enjoy something so much, I would have done it before I was the ripe old age of 27. Mark and I took our time starting a family. We enjoyed being married for five years before Malyn came along. Being a mom has been the best thing I have ever done, and I cherish every small mom moment. When Malyn was two, we started to discuss having more children. I would be ready and Mark wouldn't. Then Mark would be ready and I wouldn't. Finally, we got on the same page and I decided to go to the doctor for one final check. It was discovered that I had cancer. I knew we were done having kids.

The first surgery went well, and recovery took about a day. I had a rare form of cancer that most women don't get, and my only option was a hysterectomy. We said a final farewell to having more kids. Now, this may seem pretty cut-and-dried in the way I am presenting it. Exactly. These are the facts of the outside world, but the spiritual world I lived in went to war, and what I didn't know was that God was about to have me put on hiking boots for this next walk, because He needed to strengthen me for the rest of my life.

The spiritual battle involved mistrust, hurt and betrayal. I wanted to know why God had not trusted us with another child. Why were we going to be left out of having multiple little bodies running around the house? There would be no son to carry on the Holmen name. There would be no sounds of laughter (and fighting) from siblings playing at our house. Finally, there was nothing I could do about it. This decision had been made for us, and I felt let down by God. To me, God had done this to punish us, and I didn't like it and I didn't get it. Hadn't we done all that we were supposed to? Weren't we currently doing the best to follow the decrees and laws that had been given to us? So what's up with all of this? Why? Why? Why?

Mom Moments for You

- Have you ever gone through a life-changing experience?
- How do you handle yourself in crisis situations? Have you ever wondered why?
- What was some of the advice or counsel you received at the time?

Big Questions

In my standard Maria way, I did not talk to anyone about my spiritual battle. For almost a year I let it

build and seethe inside of me. I will say I had some
mighty good knock-down, drag-outs with God, but
I never won; and so a bitter shell of the person I
used to be emerged. Surly and cantankerous would
be good descriptors.

One cold Minnesota February night, Mark and
I were traveling back from our monthly couple's
Bible study, and he turned off the radio and asked a
gentle, genuine question, "When is the old Maria
going to come back?" I thought I had been doing a
mighty fine job keeping it all together. I had plowed
through the surgery, thrown myself into my child,
work and home and tried to be supportive of how
Mark was doing with all we had been going through.
But I must have failed, and Mark could tell that it
was affecting my walk with God. There was a part of
me that wanted to get really mad at the question
Mark had just asked me, and I wanted to defend
myself. Instead I felt incredible sadness. We had a
45-minute ride, and we spent the whole time talking about the questions I had laid out before God.
Out of all the questions, the one about God's hand
in all of this was the most frustrating; and in the
end, it gave me the most peace.

When I asked why God had done this to us,
Mark realized a huge issue needed to be resolved. I
had always believed that if you led a good life, God
would bless you; and if you didn't, God would cause
bad things to happen to you. Therefore, because
something bad had happened to us, we must have

done something to deserve it, and I didn't understand what we had done that was so bad that He
would not let us have another child. That's when
the big revelation happened where my whole relationship with God did a 180-degree turn. In a moment that was truly led by the Holy Spirit, Mark
was able to explain to me that God loved me un-
conditionally, no matter what, with no strings at-
tached. His forgiveness was always there and He
always wanted the very best for me. Always! And
then Mark dropped the bomb on me when he said,
"Did you ever think that it might not have been
God that caused this bad thing to happen but instead Satan?" Mark went on to explain that God
isn't in the business of doing the bad things. This
was Satan's job. Well, Satan was not someone I
talked about or even thought about. He didn't exist
to me, because I really didn't want to acknowledge
"the bad guy." He was not real to me like God was.

God gave Mark the words he needed for that
night. They were simple and wonderful. This was
Satan's attempt to get us to turn away from God, to
disrupt the good things God was about to do in our
lives. Mark describes it, "throwing flour on the in-
visible man moment." It was time for me to "see"
Satan because there is a lot of power in a force that
is unseen. Just as there is a real God who wants the
best for you, there is also a real Satan who can cause
bad things to happen to you in an attempt to take
you away from the promises God has made to you.

God instructs us to "be self-controlled and alert. Your enemy the devil prowls around like a roaring lion looking for someone to devour. Resist him, standing firm in the faith, because you know that your brothers throughout the world are undergoing the same kind of sufferings" (1 Peter 5:8-9).

All this made sense, but I had a final question that I needed to have answered. The big question. If it were Satan who was trying to disrupt our lives so we would turn away from God, then why would God allow Satan to do this if He loved us so much? Mark's answer was "free will." Without free will our love for God is not genuine.

You can command your kids to love you, but unless they really have the freedom to love you or not love you, it's not love. Free will is only real if there are options. We can choose to obey God or not. We can choose to love or not. The choice is *always* there. That is the true gift God has given. And free will is what, unfortunately, allows Satan in; and yet it is also what defeats Satan time and time again when we choose God.

Even though it was well after midnight when we finally stepped from the car, I felt like I could go out dancing until dawn. I was light as a feather. Freedom from this spiritual weight had been lifted and the final pieces to this cancer mystery had been answered. I could now see how Satan was working; which then made it easier for me to love and live my life fully for God. God didn't cause my cancer. He joined me in my battle with cancer; and when I cried, God cried with me. I knew from then on that God would always be there for me, and I could trust Him to lead my life fully. And from that day forward, we have been on one of the most challenging and exhilarating rides of our lives.

Mom Moments for You

- What big questions do you have that you don't seem to find answers to?
- What advice would you give to someone with big questions?

Fitting the Pieces Together

So now let's connect the dots. In the future, when your son asks you, " 'What is the meaning of the stipulations, decrees and laws the LORD our God has commanded you?' tell him . . . 'Before our eyes the LORD sent miraculous signs and wonders—great and terrible—upon Egypt and Pharaoh and his whole household' " (Deuteronomy 6:20-22). Our family battle with cancer was one of our "miraculous signs and wonders—great and terrible" all wrapped up in one. On the journey of life with your kids, you share what you have experienced—talking, asking and answering questions along the way about the miraculous signs and wonders, great and terrible—that have happened. That is what being a faith-at-home focused mom is.

One of the things I hated the most when I was dealing with cancer was when people would say to me, "Well, you just don't know what God is doing with this, but it will be revealed. Maybe not here on earth, but in heaven for sure." I would be polite and say thank you or okay, but my heart was broken. What I really wanted to say was, "Please don't talk to me if that is what you are going to say." Yes, my head knew that only God knows how much, and when, He is going to reveal things to us, but my heart didn't want to be reminded of that. The human side of us would like to have all the pieces to the puzzle now so we can feel better. So we can justify that this was all done for a greater purpose. Yet sometimes we just have to sit and wait.

It is kind of like Job who loved God deeply, yet he went through some unbelievable drama that tested his loyalty to God. When his friends showed up, what did they do? They simply sat with him. Did they sit with him for a couple of hours? No. They sat in silence with him for *days*. They knew he was in great pain and the last thing he needed was a whole bunch of talking. He simply needed time. Time to heal, time to regroup, time to cry, time to be angry and time to pick up the pieces and trust God again.

As a mom, you are going to face similar times. You are going to face times when you don't have the answers or understand why. And it's in these times that the statement, "He brought us out from there to bring us in and give us the land that he promised on oath to our forefathers" (Deuteronomy 6:23), comes into play. Is Satan at work trying to seek and destroy your relationship with God by causing all sorts of pain and turmoil in your life? Yes. We are in a spiritual war (see Ephesians 6:12). Yet, through it, is God at work bringing you out of that and into something greater that He has promised to you? Absolutely! When your children ask you, "Why, Mom?" Tell them. Tell them there is a good God and an evil Satan who are both at work. Teach them that God in you is greater than Satan working in the world (see 1 John 4:4). Show them that others before you have gone through trials, and God pulled them through and delivered them. He promises to do the same with you. Tell them that you are not the first, nor will you be the last, to face hard times. This is something that goes with the territory as Christ-followers. Jesus said there would be trials (see John 16:33). And He promised never to leave you alone (see Hebrews 13:5). Teach your children that trials can either lead you away from God or turn you ever closer to God.

One of the greatest joys I now have is to be able to talk with my daughter openly and honestly about the sadness and gladness my experience with cancer has brought me. I'm able to use this experience to tell her that there is a very real Satan who causes very real pain and suffering in an attempt to lead us away from God. I'm able to explain to her that I was tempted to turn from God because Satan was lying to me, telling me that God had given me cancer because of something I had done wrong. And then I'm able to tell her about our good, loving and compassionate God who has been with me every step of the way. I'm able to tell her that God has delivered me from this cancer and blessed me in ways that I never imagined possible nor deserved. And while I never, at the time, believed this would be possible, I am now able to tell her that I now see the experience as a good thing and that if I had to do it all over again I would do it without hesitation.

Mom, in the future, when your son or daughter asks why, tell them.

Mom Moments for You

- What are some things you need to remember that God has done for you and your family? Make a list, and don't forget the small stuff!
- Have you ever see how God has turned some-thing evil into something good?
- When your son or daughter asks you a difficult "God" question, what are you going to say or do?

Final Thoughts

I would like to talk one final time about obedience. The word "Deuteronomy" means "repetition of the law," and that's really what being a faith-at-home focused mom is all about. Repetitiously obeying the will and commands of God. The last section of Deuteronomy 6:24-25 states, "The LORD commanded us to obey all these decrees and to fear the LORD our God, so that we might always prosper and be kept alive, as is the case today. And if we are careful to obey all this law before the LORD our God, as he has commanded us, that will be our righteousness."

Moses is now asking, "So are you going to do it?" He has spelled it all out, showed the way and painted the picture of things to come. He has motivated his listeners by telling them if they obey, they will prosper; and he repeated it several times. Now, are you going to do it? Are you going to be careful to obey?

Consider your decision to obey from the perspective of who has the control. Obedience really comes down to giving up control. God is asking you one final time with this verse to obediently give up control and let Him drive. He wants to take that steering wheel and guide you to all the promises He has in store for you. He doesn't want you to sit in the driver's seat and help Him. He doesn't want you to be the backseat driver. He just wants you to ride along with Him and let Him be in control.

My mom and I were talking recently about our control issues, and she shared a great quote: "When you try to control a situation, the only person you are thinking about is you!" Love that. The decision to obey and give up control is to think beyond yourself. Remember, the decision to obey God will impact not only you but also your children and grandchildren. God knows more than you. God sees beyond what you can see. God wants what is best for you, your children and your grandchildren. God wants you to enjoy long, everlasting life. How selfish would it be to stay in control thinking only of yourself! God is telling you that He is willing to do the majority of the work if you stop trying to make it all go your way. When you give up the control, you get to live in the "righteousness" of it all.

What does that mean? Surely it is "Best Mom" awards piled up in the corner, right? Nope. It is going to bed each night wrapped in the knowledge that you have done the "right" things according to the decrees and laws of God. At the end of the day, ask yourself, "Have I obeyed God and followed His ways today?" If the answer is no, give it to God and start fresh again tomorrow. Then that's all you can do. The rest is in His hands. The only recognition you need is to hear is from the only One who can say, "Well done, good and faithful servant."

Our journey in these pages is about to end. But our parenting journey continues. Remember to continue to take "mom moments" to reflect on what

God is doing and what He wants to do in you and your family. Continue to pass along to your children faith in God and His ways. For that is what enjoying long life is all about!

Mom Moments for You

- What is your greatest hope for your child?
- What are you willing to do so that your child will enjoy eternal, life?
- What do you need to let go of so God can be in the driver's seat of your life?

Acknowledgments

I have to start with thanking my Lord and Savior, Jesus Christ, who speaks through me daily and is the true author of this resource. Without this spiritual journey, there would be no story. Thank you to Gospel Light for taking a chance with me, and for supporting the Faith@Home ministry. Thank you to Jean Lawson for doing the hard work of editing this so others can understand His Word through me. Finally, I want to thank my husband and daughter for all they did to help me with this resource. We have yet another story to laugh about because of this project. Thanks for your unconditional hard-working love!

MARIA & MARK HOLMEN

Maria and Mark Holmen, having served for more than 15 years in congregational ministry, now serve as missionaries to the Faith@Home movement. The Faith@Home movement is a national and international movement focused on equipping individuals and the Church to establish the home as the primary place where faith is nurtured. To find out more about the Faith@Home movement, visit www.faithathome.com. Maria is available to speak to parents and mom's groups. Please contact her at maria@faithathome.com.

Also Available from
Mark Holmen

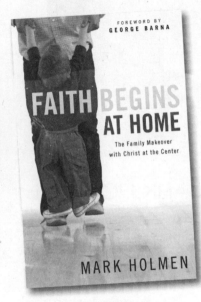

In *Faith Begins at Home*, Mark Holmen shows how becoming the strong, joy-filled and healthy family that God intended begins with parents establishing their homes as the primary place where faith is nurtured. In this engaging book, you will learn about the importance of your and your spouse's walk with the Lord; of using the gifts and experiences of grandparents, elders and mentors in the family; and of the role the church should play with families. Filled with a wealth of practical ideas, inspirational stories and biblical truth, *Faith Begins at Home* will inspire, motivate and equip you to help your family succeed.

Faith Begins at Home
ISBN 978.08307.38137
ISBN 08307.38134